INTERNATIONAL OUTBREAKS

COVID-19

Heather C. Hudak

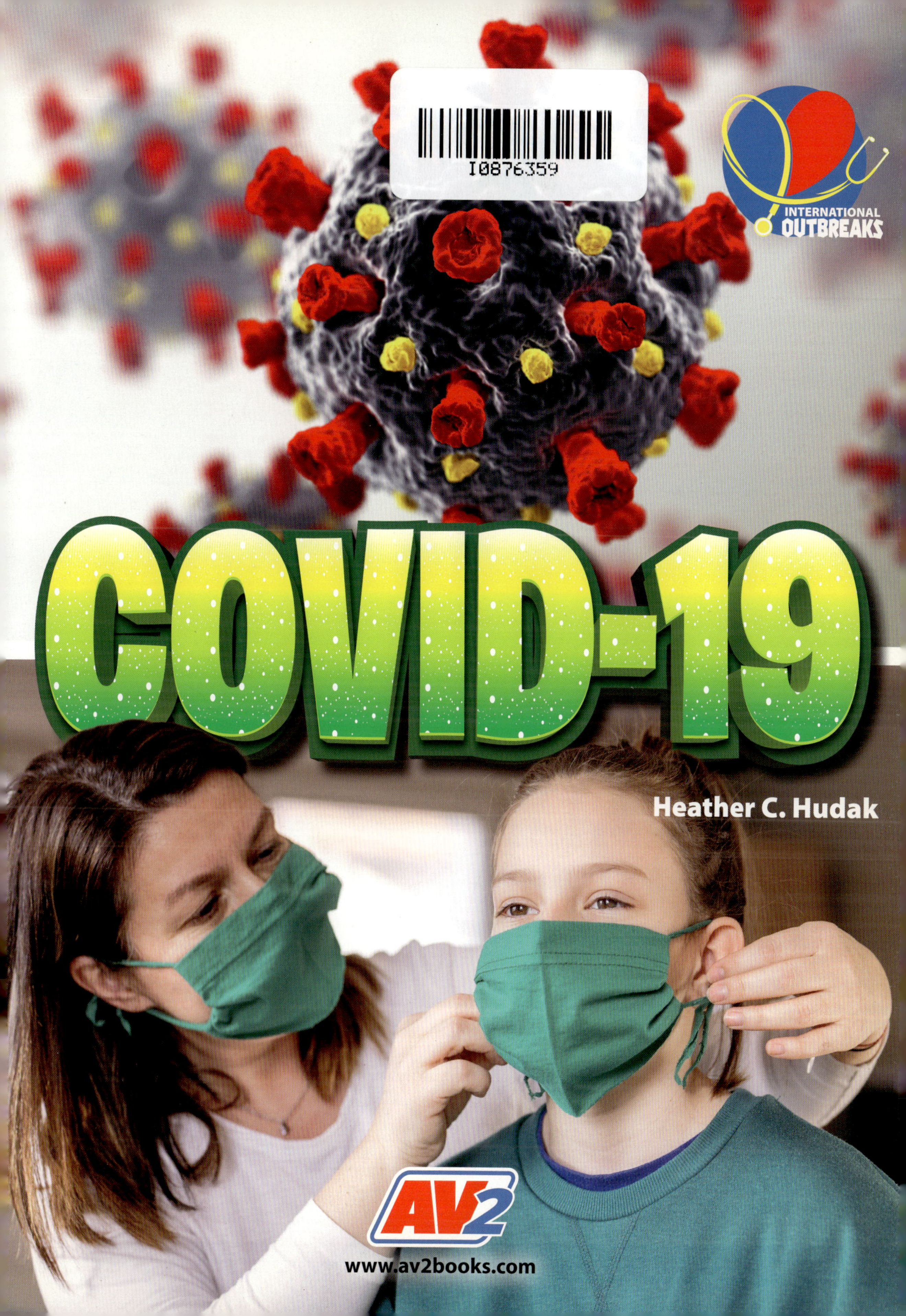

AV2
www.av2books.com

AV2

Step 1
Go to **www.av2books.com**

Step 2
Enter this unique code
YHIATA760

Step 3
Explore your interactive eBook!

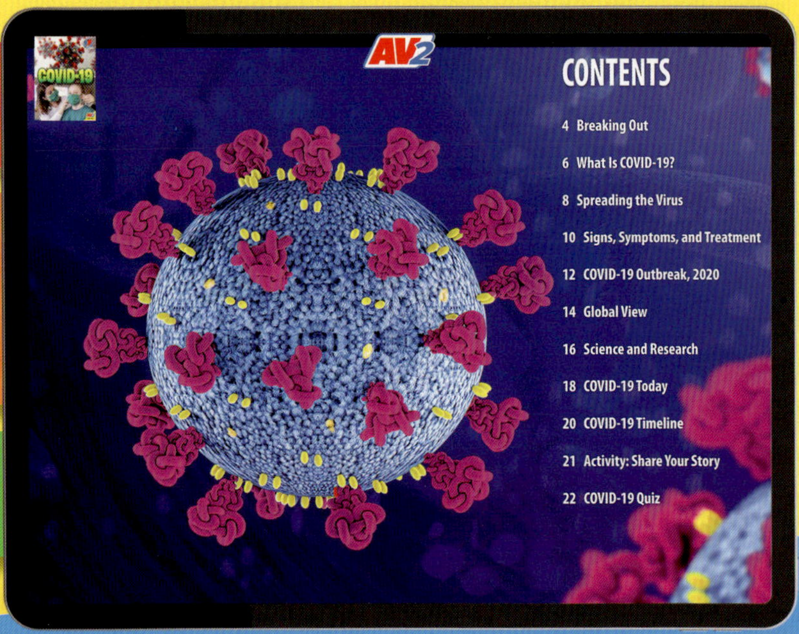

AV2 is optimized for use on any device

Your interactive eBook comes with...

Contents
Browse a live contents page to easily navigate through resources

Audio
Listen to sections of the book read aloud

Videos
Watch informative video clips

Weblinks
Gain additional information for research

Try This!
Complete activities and hands-on experiments

Key Words
Study vocabulary, and complete a matching word activity

Quizzes
Test your knowledge

Slideshows
View images and captions

... and much, much more!

INTERNATIONAL OUTBREAKS

COVID-19

CONTENTS

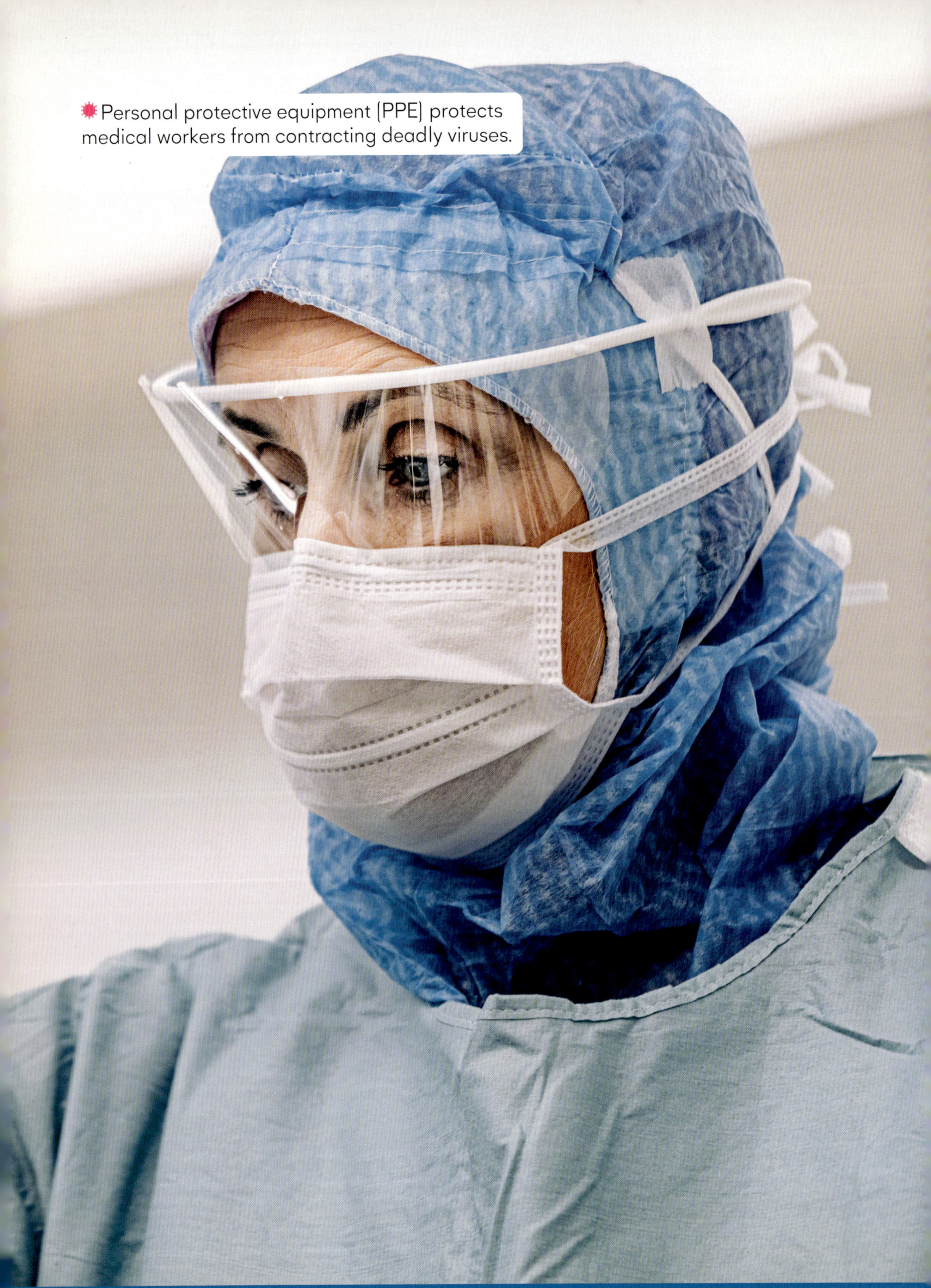

Personal protective equipment (PPE) protects medical workers from contracting deadly viruses.

Breaking Out

Diseases are all around us. Scientists track how many people normally get the same disease at a certain time and place each year. Sometimes, there are more cases than scientists expect. This is called an outbreak.

Outbreaks happen when many people are **infected** with the same disease in a short time. An outbreak can get out of control if the disease is not **contained**. A sudden increase in the number of cases is called an epidemic. Over time, the disease may even spread to several countries. A disease that affects many people around the world is called a pandemic. During a pandemic, a disease spreads quickly and causes many hardships. This is what happened in 2020. A new disease called coronavirus disease 2019, or COVID-19, led to a global pandemic.

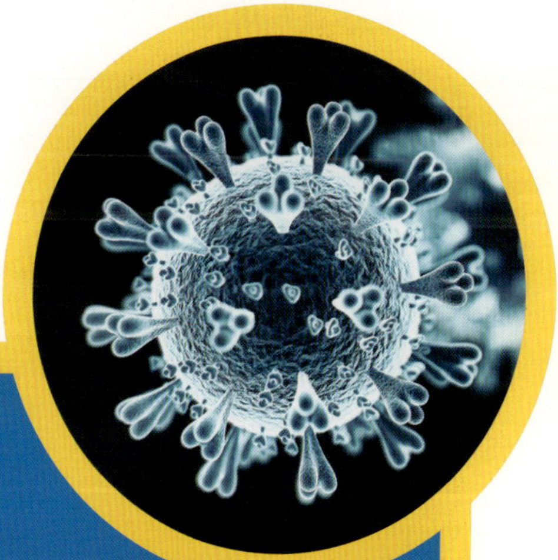

FAST FACT

The name *COVID-19* comes from a mix of words. "CO" is for *corona,* which means "crown" in Latin. The **virus** that causes COVID-19 has crown-like spikes on its surface. "VI" stands for "virus," and "D" is for "disease." The number 19 represents 2019, the year the virus was first seen.

COVID-19 can cause a fever. Temperature checks are sometimes used to try and detect COVID-19.

What Is COVID-19?

COVID-19 is caused by a family of viruses known as coronaviruses. Many types of diseases are caused by coronaviruses. The common cold is one of them. COVID-19 is caused by a new type of coronavirus. The first cases of COVID-19 took place in Wuhan, China, in late 2019. The virus quickly spread to countries all over the world.

COVID-19 can give people flu-like symptoms. The virus may cause serious problems and even death. The risks are higher for adults above the age of 40. COVID-19 is especially harmful for elderly people. People with other health conditions also face a greater **threat**. Those with diabetes, heart disease, or lung disease are more at risk.

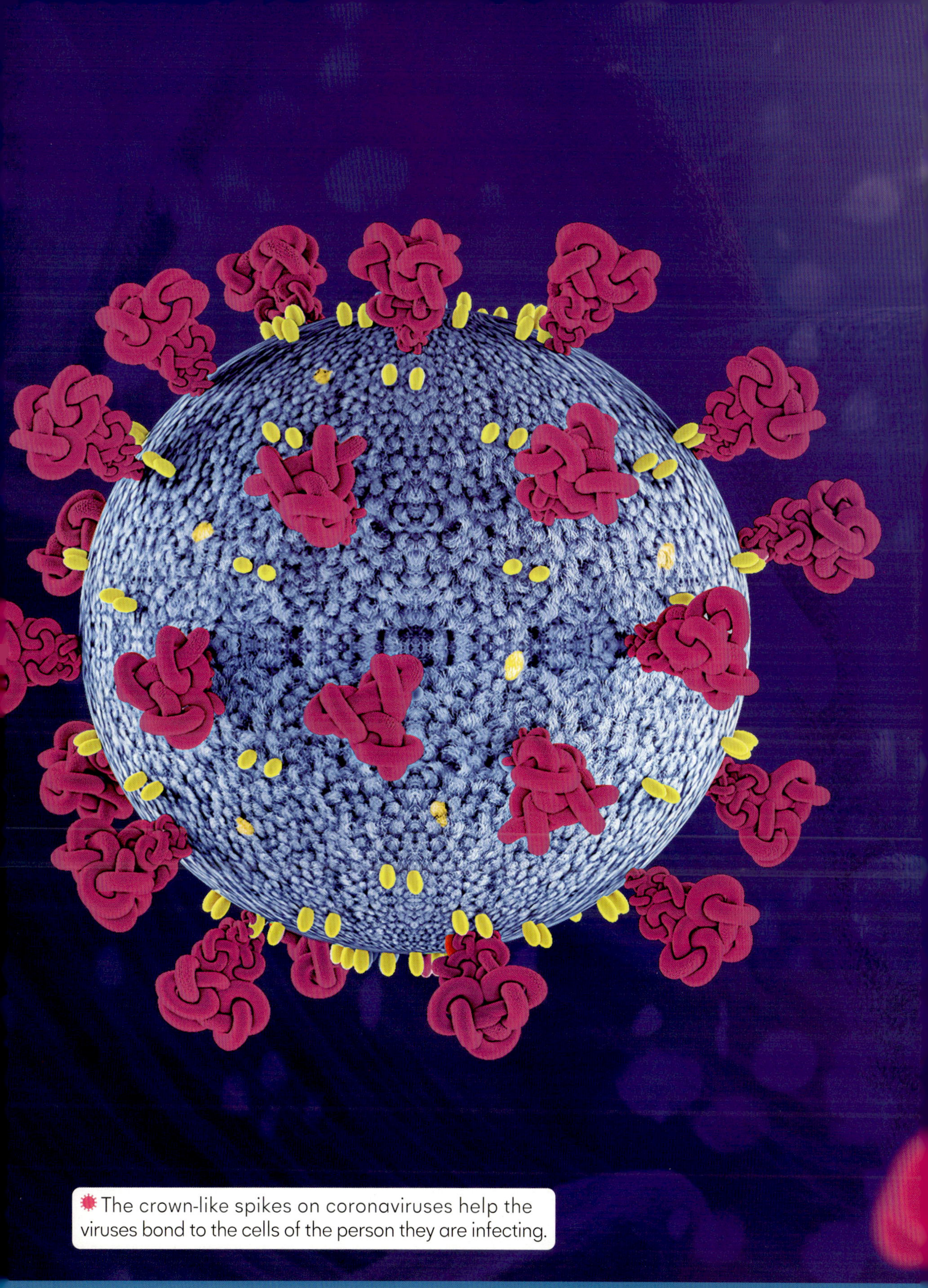

The crown-like spikes on coronaviruses help the viruses bond to the cells of the person they are infecting.

Many places began requiring people to wear masks on airplanes, trains, and buses when COVID-19 reached pandemic status.

Spreading the Virus

Anyone can get COVID-19. The virus is very **contagious**. It spreads quickly between people. Scientists do not know for certain where the virus came from. They think the first person to get it may have come in contact with an infected wild animal. However, there is no **evidence** that dogs, cats, or other pets can give a person COVID-19.

COVID-19 can spread through close contact with an infected person. Hugging, shaking hands, or sharing food are examples of close contact. COVID-19 mainly spreads through droplets that come out of an infected person's nose and mouth when he or she coughs, sneezes, or talks. The droplets then move through the air. They can get inside another person's eyes, nose, or mouth. Droplets can also land on objects, such as smartphones, door knobs, and remote controls. People may become infected if they touch an object with droplets on it and then touch their eyes, nose, or mouth.

Staying 6 feet (2 meters) away from other people and wearing a mask can help prevent the COVID-19 virus from spreading.

Staying Safe

Many diseases are caused by viruses. Scientists discovered the first virus known to infect humans in 1901. It was the yellow fever virus. There are many different types of viruses on Earth, but there are only 219 viruses presently known to infect humans. Scientists discover three or four new human viruses each year.

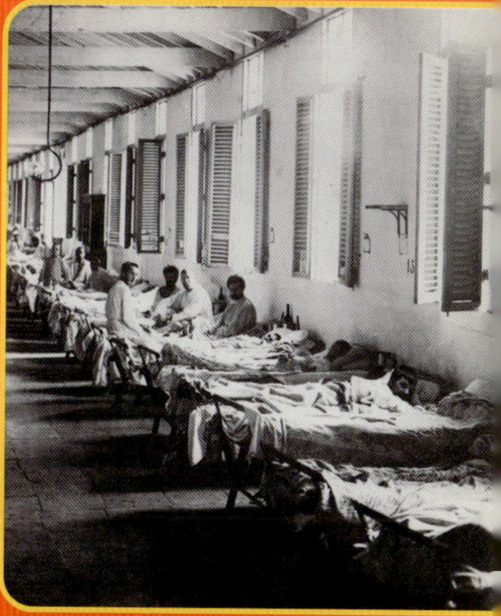

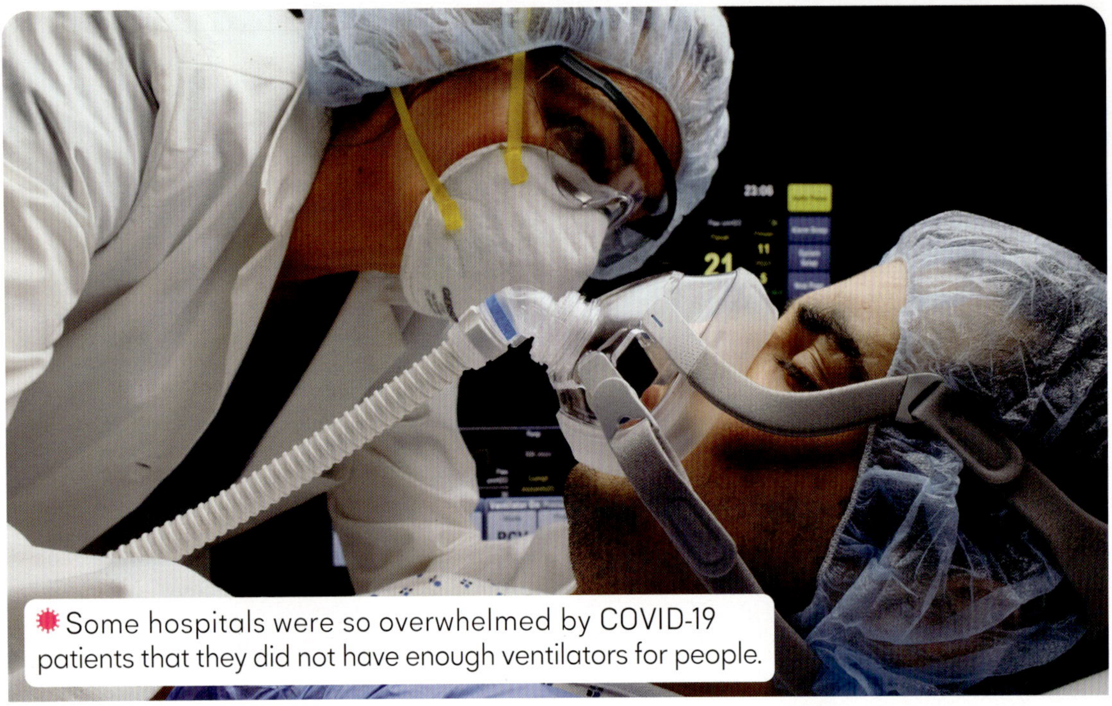

Some hospitals were so overwhelmed by COVID-19 patients that they did not have enough ventilators for people.

Signs, Symptoms, and Treatment

Most people show signs of COVID-19 about five or six days after they get the virus. However, symptoms can appear as soon as two days after infection and up to 14 days later. Common symptoms include fever, cough, and breathing problems. Some people have a sore throat, a stuffy or runny nose, chills, muscle pain, and headaches. They may vomit, have diarrhea, or lose their senses of smell and taste. Some people who get COVID-19 do not show any signs at all. They can still pass the virus on to others.

There is no known cure or treatment for COVID-19. Most people with COVID-19 have mild symptoms. The symptoms go away on their own after one or two weeks of rest. Other people are treated for their symptoms. People with severe symptoms must stay in the hospital. They may need help from a **ventilator** to breathe.

Prevent COVID-19 by Protecting Yourself and Others

Wash your hands often

Use alcohol-based hand sanitizer

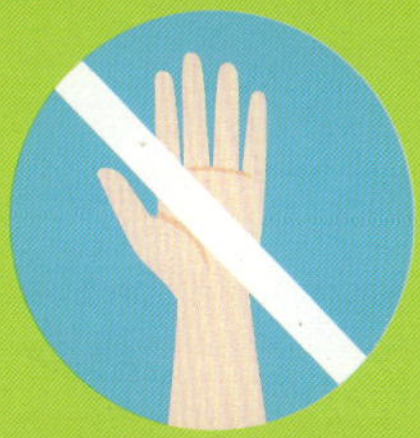

Avoid touching your eyes, nose, or mouth with unwashed hands

Wear a mask

Cover coughs and sneezes with a tissue

Cough or sneeze into your elbow if you do not have tissue

Avoid close contact with people who are sick

Stay home if you are sick

Avoid large groups of people

Clean and disinfect objects and surfaces

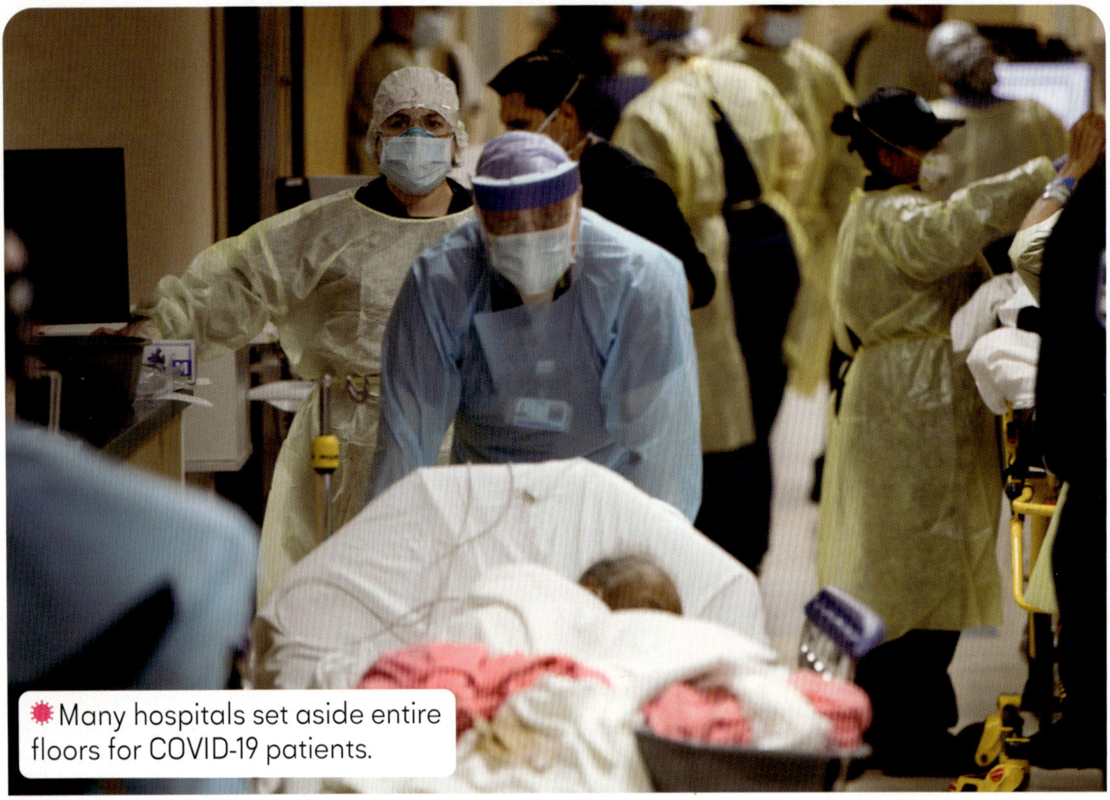

Many hospitals set aside entire floors for COVID-19 patients.

COVID-19 Outbreak, 2020

On December 31, 2019, health officials in China announced that dozens of people were sick with a new type of pneumonia. They did not think the disease could spread from person to person at the time.

The first case appeared in the United States less than a month later. There were also cases reported in Japan, Thailand, and South Korea at about the same time. On January 30, 2020, the **World Health Organization** (WHO) declared a global health emergency.

Mapping the COVID-19 Outbreak on January 30, 2020

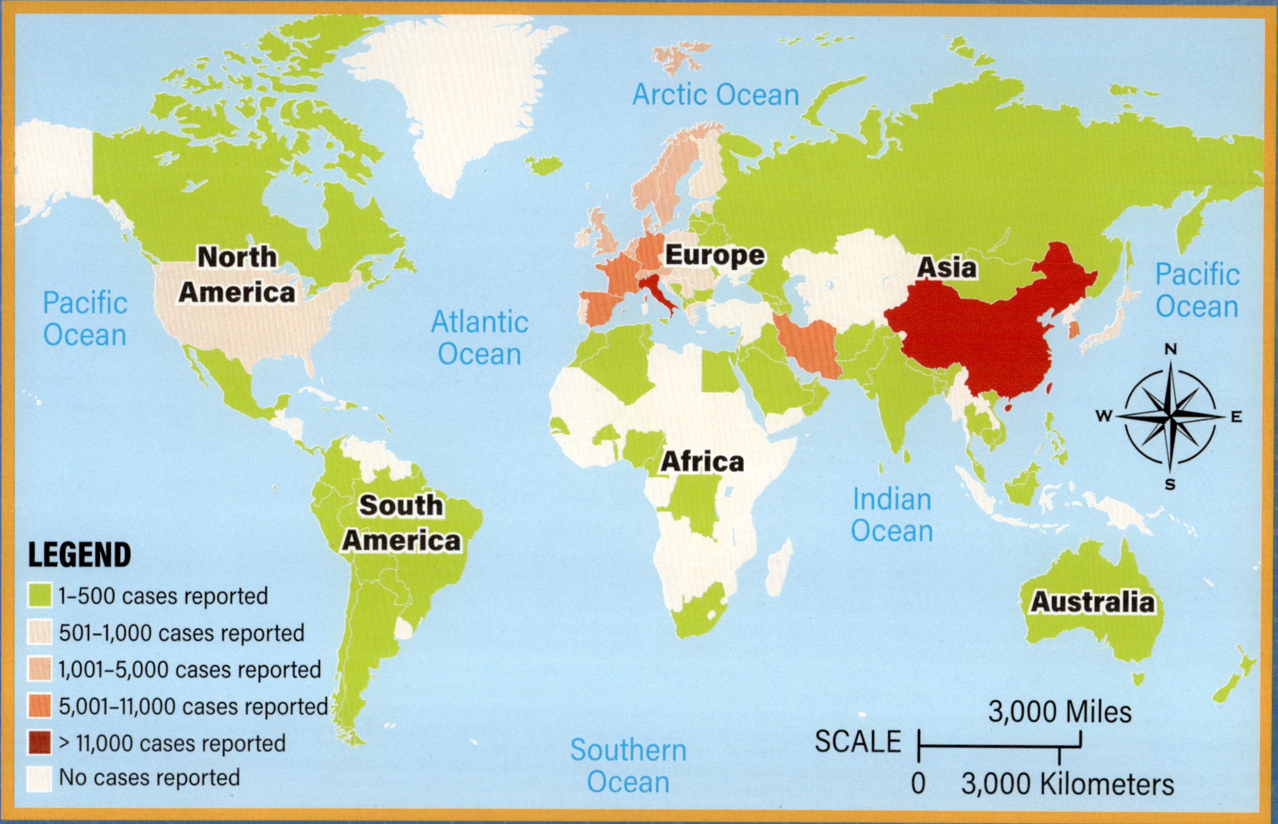

COVID-19 was **first detected** in China in **December 2019** and spread through travel.

By **January 2020**, COVID-19 was **rapidly spreading through Europe**.

Due to a **rapid increase in the number of cases**, many parts of the world started **lockdowns** and closed public spaces by **March 2020**.

Millions of people worked from home for the first time during the COVID-19 pandemic. Video conferencing became increasingly widespread.

Global View

On March 11, 2020, WHO officially declared COVID-19 a pandemic. Nearly the entire world shut down. Schools and businesses closed. Many people worked from home. Children had to do schoolwork at home. Only essential services stayed open to allow people to buy necessary items such as groceries and fuel.

Most countries closed their borders. Flights between countries stopped. People were told to remain in their homes. Still, millions became ill. Hospitals were overrun with sick people in many parts of the world. Health workers did not have enough masks, gloves, and gowns to protect themselves. There were not enough ventilators and supplies to treat everyone. Hundreds of thousands of people died. The number of new cases started to drop in some countries, but went up in others.

Different Points of View

Countries took different approaches to dealing with the COVID-19 pandemic. Many disagreed with how other countries handled the crisis. Some countries worked together to support one another. It is important to learn about different perspectives on an issue. Listening to other points of view helps people see the world in a new way.

Science and Research

Scientists around the world are working hard to find a **vaccine** for COVID-19. Doctors and researchers are also looking for medicines and other ways to treat people. For now, the only way for people to protect themselves from COVID-19 is to prevent its spread.

Good hygiene is the best way to stop the spread of any virus. People should wash their hands often. They should not touch their eyes, nose, and mouth when they are out in public. This helps stop the COVID-19 virus from getting into their bodies. People should use the bend of their elbow or a tissue to cover their mouth when they cough or sneeze. Social distancing is also important.

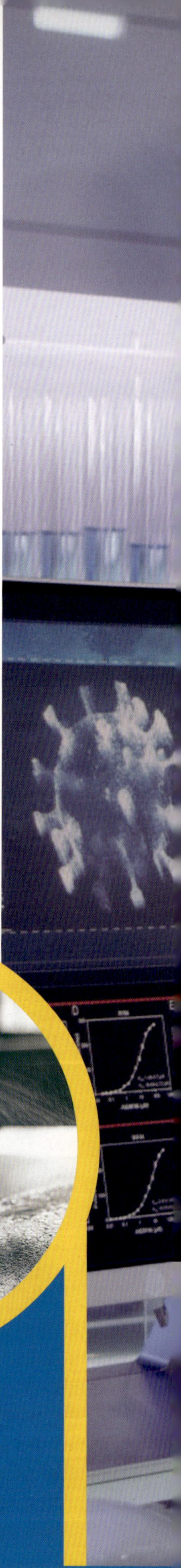

FAST FACT

Scientists believe that the COVID-19 virus can live on objects made from plastic and stainless steel for up to 72 hours. It lives for less than 24 hours on cardboard and no more than 4 hours on copper. Using disinfectants to clean surfaces that people touch helps get rid of any germs.

Vaccines can take months or even years to develop and test before they are safe to use on people.

Businesses that reopen must have proper social distancing procedures.

COVID-19 Today

COVID-19 is still a major concern, but most countries started to reopen by the summer of 2020. They needed to start making money again to help the **economy** recover. Each community put rules in place to help stop COVID-19 from spreading. For example, shops and restaurants could only let in a certain number of people at a time. In some places, COVID-19 cases became worse after businesses reopened. Those places had to close again to help stop the spread.

The future of COVID-19 is uncertain. There are still thousands of new cases each day. People are reminded of COVID-19 every time they step outside and must keep their distance from others. However, each day, scientists learn more about the virus and how to keep people safe. Keeping up to date on the latest facts is a good way to stay hopeful.

COVID-19 in the United States by June 30, 2020

COVID-19 Timeline

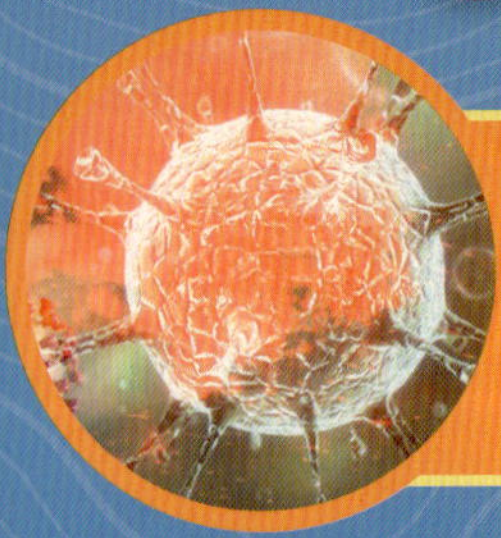

December 31, 2019
A mysterious new disease causes dozens of people to fall ill in Wuhan, China.

January 7, 2020
Scientists discover the cause of the disease is a new type of coronavirus.

January 20, 2020
The disease spreads to Japan, Thailand, and South Korea.

January 21, 2020
The disease appears in the United States.

February 11, 2020
The new disease is officially named COVID-19.

March 11, 2020
WHO officially declares COVID-19 a pandemic.

June 30, 2020
Nearly 10 million COVID-19 cases are reported worldwide. The death toll reaches more than 500,000 people.

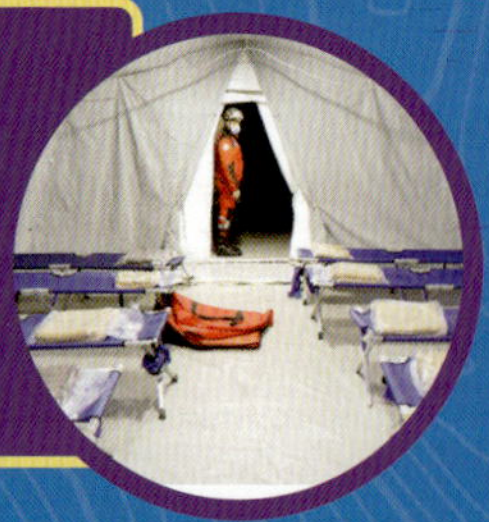

ACTIVITY
Share Your Story

Did you have to stay at home during the COVID-19 pandemic? Think about all the ways COVID-19 changed your life. Then, look for ways to share your story with others. Try one of these ideas to record your daily experiences, thoughts, and feelings.

- **Cut out magazine and newspaper clippings**
- **Collect objects and items**
- **Take photos**
- **Keep a journal**
- **Start a YouTube channel with your parents' permission**
- **Draw pictures**

Once you choose how to tell your story, be sure to include plenty of details.

1. What was it like to go into isolation? What did you do? Perhaps you played games with your family or went on hikes in nature.
2. How did you feel? Were you afraid? Did you miss your friends? How did you keep in touch with them?
3. What gave you hope for the future? What acts of kindness did you do or see?

COVID-19 QUIZ

1
When were the first cases of COVID-19 discovered?

2
Where was the first COVID-19 outbreak?

3
How does COVID-19 spread?

4
When did scientists discover the first virus known to infect humans?

5
Who can get COVID-19?

6
How can people stop the spread of COVID-19?

7
How many cases of COVID-19 were reported in the United States by June 30, 2020?

8
When was COVID-19 declared a pandemic?

ANSWERS

1. Late 2019
2. Wuhan, China
3. Through droplets from an infected person
4. In 1901
5. Anyone
6. By maintaining physical distance from others, wearing a mask, and washing their hands or using hand sanitizer often
7. 2,537,636
8. March 11, 2020

Key Words

contagious: moves easily from one person to another

contained: kept under control

diseases: illnesses that have certain signs and symptoms

economy: the wealth and resources of a country or how much money a country makes or loses

evidence: facts or proof that something is true

infected: contaminated a person or object with a disease-causing germ

threat: something that is likely to cause damage or harm

vaccine: a substance made from a small amount of a disease-causing germ to help provide immunity against that germ

ventilator: a device that helps people breathe by moving air in and out of their lungs

virus: a very small germ that gets inside the body and spreads

World Health Organization: an organization that sets health standards and guidelines that many countries follow

Index

Published by AV2
14 Penn Plaza, 9th Floor
New York, NY 10122
Website: www.av2books.com

Library of Congress Control Number: 2020943888

ISBN 978-1-7911-3230-9 (hardcover)
ISBN 978-1-7911-3231-6 (softcover)
ISBN 978-1-7911-3232-3 (multi-user eBook)
ISBN 978-1-7911-3233-0 (single-user eBook)

Printed in Guangzhou, China
1 2 3 4 5 6 7 8 9 0 24 23 22 21 20

082020
101119

Art Director: Terry Paulhus Project Coordinator: Priyanka Das

The publisher acknowledges Getty Images, iStock, and Shutterstock as its primary image suppliers for this title.